The Silhouettes

Lily Ladewig

SpringGun Press / Denver, Colorado / 2012

The Silhouettes

Published by SpringGun Press
Denver, Colorado
www.springgunpress.com

The Silhouettes
©2012 by Lily Ladewig

Printed in the United States of America

ISBN 978-0-9832218-1-4

Cover art and design by Erin Costello

Generous funding for this publication
has been provided through private donations.
Special thanks to Wendy and Gary Rockswold
who believe in SpringGun's mission to promote
dialogue and community in the arts.

Distributed to the trade by Small Press Distribution
(spdbooks.org)

ACKNOWLEDGMENTS

Grateful acknowledgment is made to the editors of the following publications where versions of these poems first appeared: *Conduit, Denver Quarterly, Drunken Boat, H_NGM_N, Horse Less Review, Ink Node, Jellyroll, OmniVerse, Pax Americana, Salt Hill, So and So, SUPERMACHINE, Thermos,* and *Word For/Word.*

"Poem for You" and "Another Poem for You" were published as part of a chapbook entitled *You Are My Favorite Person of the Year* by Mondo Bummer Books, 2010.

Selections from the "Shadow Box" series will appear in the anthology *narrative dis(continuities): prose experiments by younger american writers,* edited by Kristina Marie Darling, forthcoming from Moria Books in 2012.

I am deeply grateful to Dara Wier, James Tate, Peter Gizzi, Lisa Olstein, Matthew Rohrer, and Deborah Digges who encouraged me through their teaching and writing. Thank you as well to Erin Costello and Mark Rockswold who had faith in this book and were so wonderful to work with. Loving gratitude to Megan Fishmann, who, at seventeen, convinced me that we would one day be published writers. Finally, a big thank you to the friends who sat across from me in libraries, coffee shops, and kitchens while I wrote these poems: Anne, the Bens, the Brians, Christy, David, Francesca, Jess, Jono, Leigh, Lesley, and Seth.

CONTENTS

for my parents,
James Ladewig
& Jane Bernstein

Elegance is refusal.

Coco Chanel

Sadness plus finance equals luxury.

Ana Božičević

I Didn't Come Here to Make Friends

I came here to swim. If we spend a day
driving to a stream but end up inside

a house. I look out the windows to the woods
across the stream but cannot see the water.

It's like I'm far away from it or in a field
somewhere. If I nap I dream of rabbits.

Specifically the process of cooking them.
Love, will you shake the branches or chop

the celery? The windows darken and soon
they mirror us. If I forgot to pack enough books

and my lacy underthings. If we close our eyes
and hear the water. If you make an apple and

cheese sandwich. Between bites I use my tongue
to push little pink pieces back between

the slices of bread. You give me little pink star-shaped
pills and if I ask what they are you say *pink stars*.

On Silhouettes

1. an outline of somebody or something filled in with black or a dark color on a light background, especially when done as a likeness or a work of art

The year is 1759. All of Paris is wearing itchy periwigs. Étienne de Silhouette is the King's new financial minister, which is to say he's a very important tax collector. You bump into him at parties everywhere. Try speaking. When you say *Louis XV* it comes out sounding like *Louie Cans*. When I said *everywhere* I meant *at Versailles*. We're in the middle of the Seven Years War and we need money. Étienne de Silhouette knows what to do. He melts down the King's gold and silver. He has the ear of the King's mistress. If I were to whisper the words *the King's influential mistress* into your ear, you would think *Madame de Pompadour*. You would be right and she's standing right over there, all the many of her in the mirrors wearing hair like snow-covered topiary. Showing off her dainty wrists to everyone. Her breasts the shape of the glass *coupes de champagne* in our hands. Étienne de Silhouette is taxing your windows, taxing your doorframes. He's so unpopular he might cry. Hiding himself in the tapestries. Blending into the stitched-in outlines of nightingales. Resigning after only nine months. From now on we'll refer to anything made on the cheap as *à la silhouette.* The portrait of a shadow of a man.

Voilà

I am there. It is like fall
outside. Outside

in my insomnia,
the tornado that hit

Brooklyn.
The tree and the car.

Do you follow? Do you
think of me sometimes?

For you I am perfecting
my liquid line. I stole that

line. Do you know
how many people have told me

that I have a *lovely figure?*
I have lost count. In the fall

I go to sports bars and pretend
to understand football.

I send a text message to everyone
I've ever met saying

Happy Rocktober,
gorgeous.

From Here the Coastline

is neither real nor exotic.

The way California's license plate is indicative. I've left the country.
I've lived my whole life and all of my mistakes were almost tropical.
Just the opposite.

The lake water or aquamarine.

This must be what swallowing the horizon feels like. The confusion
of faucets engraved *C & F.*

The light diffusing and some microorganisms in there. Like widows.
We go about our business without umbrellas like so many medieval
villages perched.

*

Or this small vase full of fat roses (pale pink, dark pink, reddish-pink)
sitting on the balcony for four cold hours. I'm trying to be as elegant
about this as possible. Tallow-yellow.

Repeated *olive grove,*

olive grove, olive grove to tarnish its romance.

*

In another life I was that nameless church lit up at night,
halfway up the mountainside.
I am trying

to be Egyptian about the whole thing, a kind of
hieroglyph. I wear it
like a necklace.

*

She said marriage to him was like a black and white foreign movie without subtitles. She pinned up the roses around the entryway.

*

Is it the coffee or the way I make it?

The importance of good water pressure cannot be overstated. I could stare at these mountains forever and still come away wordless,

napkins full of sucked-on cherry pits ringed in fruit flesh.

*

Before I left the country I almost drove us all off a bridge,

it was all so *Jules et Jim* I could barely contain myself. The car. The car stereo.

*

And would you know—my skin is the best camouflage. The big boat of a bed. I have three months to practice my hellos. Would prefer to say it on a bicycle. Hello. So nice to meet you.

Shadow Box

Let's build a fire. A shifting location. A
change of wind and I can smell myself.
Like something foreign. And into the fuller
fascination. I can see the Chrysler Building
from the window of the subway car on
the bridge. I would measure the distance
between us footwise. I would pull this
poem from you with my whole body.
Beneath your bright palms my breasts
might become a reality. While my hands,
full of acreage. Are budding outside your
open third story window. The dancers push
their painted feet across the page.

Shadow Box

I don't remember you putting even one
finger inside. Me: these burn blotches, the
dresses I wore. An example of the body. The
body wants what the body. Wants. Is it so
emblazoned? Is it possible to be in a garden
and not be in Italy? Each night we managed
to consume. Two lobsters each. Apple pie
à la mode. We embellished the margins
with the city. To wake up every morning
forgetful. City of fedoras. You might say
it was trusting but you would veer wrong.
Somewhere, the city of. Shaking bedbones.
All I want now are your birds. All of them.

Shadow Box

Have you ever seen a pecan grove? That
was the one time I've been arrested in my
life. In the wet grass like drunkards. A
fleur de lys of feeling. It was pressed. I was
kicking. The comforter. They called the
cops. I've been haunting you for hours
now. The trick is not to get too gnarled
up about it. Imagine rendering chicken
fat. Turning to you then away. The over-
turning of your turning. The tailored
shirt, for example. It can be worn tight
on the body, or totally oversized, with
tights and a pair of tall heels. I could say
what you're expecting. I could be a blond.
I could keep going.

Free Diving

There are people who dive one hundred yards down
into the ocean without breathing. It's called free diving

and they make no money doing it. It's a game
about knowing your body and the second most dangerous sport

after jumping off skyscrapers with a parachute. Did you know
that once you swim thirty meters below the surface, your body
    becomes

negatively buoyant? You naturally sink. Free divers know that
when their bodies tell them to breathe, their bodies are lying.

They know to keep holding their breath and keep pushing
through the layers of water. Yesterday I filled my bathroom sink

with ice water and put my head in. Once you put your face to cold
water something called the mammalian diving reflex kicks in

and the heartbeat slows. I was supposed to imagine that my lungs
    were lemons
but couldn't. It was all very emotional. I walked out of the house

and sat in the garden. I stared at the fat bumblebees and thought
I do not know my body because it is a liar. How bees sticking

their noses in flowers are fascinating but in your kitchen are a terror.
How sex underwater feels like flying, only better.

Elegant Monsters

To be someone's cup of tea
or a flight of stairs.

To start one's own line of fur.
What are silhouettes to the streamline.

To be a freak is to be Valentine
pattern-making against the threadbare.

To be beautiful is to be damaged:
Baudelaire undoing window-dressings.

Nightfall turned organza on us.
Like ombré on style-watch

I dreamed in ankleboots,
the mega-turbo kind with cloven

toes, your mouth a protrusion of leather.
To dress in animal parts,

we are ever-returning
to the Palais Royal as Valentine

struts the studio floor.
What are hemlines to the populace.

To be painted as Love is painted poorly.
A mandorla of mink, of happenstance.

Poem for the Clock

Last night's movie was like
catching up with old friends.

An overcast morning.
An eagle's foe

cries my name, cries
Hand over the Manolos!

For fear of wrinkling
in my sleep

I crush a moth.
In the morning

it looks like torn paper.
Old habits live strong.

It's hard to stop myself
from crossing my legs.

A ladylike ever-loving.
You text therefore I am

who I want to be—
an unwound clock in summer.

This is what happened
when I learned to ride a bike:

nothing was ever the same.
I don't know

who the eagle's foe is,
you'll have to imagine it yourself.

The Mess Around

I am an uncontained balloon
and tomorrow is February.
The rivers are frozen. The roads
are like skeletons. Gradually
my bones start evaporating.
I am carrying a heavy telephone
in my purse. There's the door.
I've been drinking too much
wild raspberry soda. I've been
putting roses in the blender again.
I go to the dog shelter I go
to the baby nursery. I think about
stealing something. Everybody
do the mess around.

On Silhouettes

2. something lit in such a way as to appear dark but surrounded by light, or the effect produced by such lighting

The way he put his hand on the back of his neck

when the phone rang. The news of it. The man who was dying

could have one day been someone's husband. Now the body

of. Photographs made to look like daguerreotypes

line the walls. Newspapers pile up under kitchen tables.

How many times have we compared the body to a map.

So often his eyes seem to say something. Words that sound

like *crepuscule*. Have we compared the body to a book.

To a bed. How you could have loved this husband. You might

have reached your arms overhead to press palms to the white wall

behind you. His shoulders like couplets. Try not to look at his torso

but imagine it. Better yet, place him against the white wall.

Stare at him for a good minute then close your eyes.

He will appear as a pale silhouette against a backdrop of rust.

Horses Dream of Horses

I don't want the body
of the thing, just the image.

That's why I carry this
invisible camera around

my neck. *Smile,*
I say, then, *Click!*

I'm taking your photo
as if I were telling you

a secret. Now
I've captured you

from multiple angles.
It's OK,

I'm collaging you
on top of a plastic motorcycle,

inside a toy taxi cab.
You are moving in many directions

at the same time. Later
I will draw pictures

of you directly
from my invisible

photographs. I'll tape them
inside a cardboard box

and float it
down the river.

Poem for Lauren Ireland

My biggest concern was how to break apart
the animal. I used knives and my hands.
I reread your telegram for inspiration and dug
my heels in. At this point I was already hungry,
I turned on the stove and threw all my wine glasses
out the window. I stuck your telegram to the fridge
with a yellow *X* magnet. The Le Creuset
was beautiful. So beautiful I turned off the lights
and put my hands on it. I closed my eyes and pressed
my face in the little animal's belly. I filled the Le
Creuset with water and placed it outside the back door
to capture the moon. I contemplated penne
versus spaghetti. Your telegram fell to the floor.
The moon was a little white leaf floating in the dark.

Shadow Box

Like I left you somewhere. On the corner
of Cumberland and Dekalb with your bike
lock and I took my umbrella. Took my
rings back. Gave you your keys back. Went
whole-heartedly to the horrible opera.
Like if a tree falls in a forest. I stopped
crying like a miracle. Like how if nobody
looks at my naked body then I will never
be truly naked again. Then what do these
reflections mean? What does my skin feel
like? Consenting. Everything I do goes
into my blue bower. I call this nesting for
attention.

Shadow Box

Let's scare you up some drama. An 18th
century peepshow. A typical entertainment
of the time period. Take a look. Through
this peephole. The dimensions pile on,
revealing a poor paint job. There I was,
fearless and standing on tables. Now I
am something vivid. You are some thing.
Seaward. What are whales? Why are whale
hunted? In my sleep I start stealing. A
puddle of pale blue on the floor. The most
delicate patch of it. In the city their hands
smell of oranges. Soon I will stop. Writing
poems about poems. I count the scratches
on your back. I name them like ships.

Shadow Box

You can always return to a room, even if it no longer exists. Even if you don't pray, there is something soothing about pressing your palms together. Bowing your head. They say that much of our decision-making is a result of biology. They say when you visit Russia you never for a moment forget that you are in Russia. I smelled you and within five seconds I knew. Nothing stays clean. Not my white t-shirts. Not your white jeans. The skin between a sailor's tattoos. I bathe and then I have to bathe again. If I keep repeating what I think I should want, I might start believing it.

Husbands & Other Seasons

It was pink of you. Texting me
like that. Going to the grocery store.

I've always thought weekends were the worst.
What to do

with myself. With my hands
at the gallery opening.

So you've created an environment
while I tease out the lines. The ways to describe it.

Devotion served hot in October. I stay up all night
baking dozens of quiches. Painting and repainting

the pink walls. The morning: an island appearing
gradually on the horizon. Something to climb into a boat for.

Poem for You

Partial nudity means never
having to say you're sorry.
You been keeping it real
like a violence. Like the devil
between us. I was born in your kitchen.
Your name is not Omolara
but you are being born all the time.
If you're not falling in love
you might as well be making a mix tape.
Making strips of paper dolls
heart-colored. You take a hold
of the scissor and snip!
So like a man, the lightening condenses.

My Midlife Crisis

And then the mold came. And then the locusts. You went from crescent moon to triangle. There were songbirds in the palapa. There were spiders and scorpions. I looked on the tree trunks as on dinosaurs and then the jeeps came. You went from half-moon to happy baby. The dogs needed bathing, were attacking each other. I missed the phone call but not the pickpockets. I macheteed the coconut, stuck a straw through it and gave it to the German. And then the rain came. The oceans were always warmer than the swimming pools. I had eight limbs, I counted them. There was never enough food. You slowly became aware of the breath. Pelicans in formation. The healer touched me and I changed my body. I was just my skeleton. There was never enough room in the taxicab. I covered myself in ash and stopped eating. You went from fish to corpse. And then the winter.

Good Winter

Winter turns me
head to knee.
It was spring
all winter or winter
all spring, it was
a tumbledown slideshow.
I memorized
every name and folded
them into paper.
The paper took them.
I love my winter
car dearly, its green
humming, its always
starting. In winter
my body is made up of many
layers to be peeled away
like a Russian
or a silkworm.
Always the cracking
of skin. In winter
see how my bliss
body is covered?
2005 was a good winter
for layering and last
winter was wrapped in red plaid but
this is the winter of many Zacharys.

I am none of these winters.

I am the silhouettes
of two girls
in black coats clicking
down a Roman side street.

Thank You

Love means never having to say *thank you* to the teakettle. The clear cold night is a soft clumsy thing, a most disagreeable intrusion. Your beard is relative. Thank you. The countertops are so clean thank you for removing your boots. Famous people die all the time regardless of whether or not you've met them, sold them a ticket to the museum, served them a stiff drink and they said *thank you, Susan.* Thank you, elderflowers. Thank you, this is such a surprise, such a lovely party. Champagne cocktails, cocktail rings. I have so many super important things to tell you about, like skirt lengths. Thank you for the oxygen. Thank you for the all the elderflowers. It's Valentine's Day and there are beautiful women all over this city. They carefully arrange themselves like static electricity on a shag carpet and they accept compliments so well.

There was a time when all women were drugged and all oranges were squeezed. We've had two amazing days of little jackets and NO TIGHTS. And look, the new colors are already here! I am a woman too and my name is Susan. It's harder to burn something than you might think. It's so cold we wear our hats indoors. Once we learned to read the book backwards, things started making sense. Thank you for this helpful hint. I'm strapping nightlights to my shoes. Thank you, weather. Drug the women and squeeze the oranges. Thank you, winter. I'm in the snow!!! I'm drinking hot chocolate!!! I'm tanning!!! I have a jumpsuit that changes colors in the sun!!!

On Silhouettes

3. the outline of a body viewed as circumscribing a mass <the silhouette of a bird>

When Peter Pan's shadow misbehaves
Wendy must sew it back onto his heels
with a needle and thread. As a fashion term
a silhouette has as much to do with the cut
and shape of a garment as it does with the body
underneath it. One might say *strong shoulders*
or *whittled waist* and that would signify. Today
we favor androgyny and from a distance
a person standing on a street corner
with their back to you might appear genderless.

Shadow Box

Our poems will never be as good as pop
songs. I dare you to dance them across the
floor on a Sunday. It's one thing to say *I
like your shoes* but it's another to say *I like
all the shoes you've ever worn.* Or *push me
up against the tree why don't you.* As the
essentials are not around, I concentrate
on the accessories. I am moving as slowly
as possible so you won't see me. An
assemblage of. What hurts where. We
didn't sleep for weeks. When we did it
was about the forsythia. This is all I ever
wanted: a room of Marie-Antoinette-blue:
a chandelier where my heart once was.

Shadow Box

You made a room and put a window in it.
I was a moving picture. Dancing to Bartok
in your storefront. There was white all
over everything outside like the memory
of snow. Where science leads we both
followed. I used sex as a kind of alchemy.
It was easy. Something base. Something
precious. Turn my body into a specimen.
A blue-colored cocktail. The room at its
most abstract. We made a mutual decision.
See this bracelet? Made of sapphires and I
think it's the most beautiful thing that I've
ever been given to wear. The most precious.

Shadow Box

For years I made a living. Making sweaters
and cakes. The square of light around. My
bedroom door. Also captivated with birds.
These boxes are meant to be handled.
My skin takes its color. Takes it all. You
continue to comment. To like. I tend to
have a favorite piece or silhouette I wear
constantly until something else catches my
eye. The city is the place where. At night-
fall our shadows turn into choreographers.
They instruct the dancers not to touch but
to imagine touching. We tried. To make
it look antique the usual practice is to
stain. The city is the place.

Templates

Call me when you get this message.

When the clouds roll in they slice the mountains.
One is backlit so as to make us believe

if you stay indoors all day you won't have to speak
French to anyone. Our little violences of the day-to-day

to ourselves and to others, you turn
the wrong corner and there you are.

When can we meet?

Put the plastic peonies on the backburner to watch them melt into.
Hot pink imperative or fragmented past tense? When did we stop
calling it the Middle West?

Where are you?

For one month I was alive and it was exhausting.
From this afternoon I watch many weather patterns:
bright sky to the left and mountain rain
to the right, then the reverse.
Clouds falling on towns.

Talk to you soon.

I take you as my reference point.
You take it lavender-like.
If I write *broke me* you will see plumage.
If I write *plumage* you will see.

I am late and will be there in _____ minutes.

And what? Wearing
my mother's wedding dress
to the rock show? An aerialist twisted
in scarves above us? Rather,
watch the rain move over the lake.
Vibrating its ruffles, cinching the foothills
where they sleep.

I am here.

plum•age *n*
1. The feathers that cover a bird's body, considered collectively.
2. Something about time and distance.

Sorry I missed your call, I am in a meeting.

Will winter become unbearable due to our mutual love of snow?

How is it going?

The steep slope of the road leads me
to believe there are people speaking French
on my balcony. The lake lit up

even in a rainstorm and suddenly, a sailboat.
Or me, bringing you ginger ale.
Like if I lost my underpants
on the roof or my shoes under the bed

and had to find my way home
barefoot. A swan
flying over soft water.

Shadow Box

What is the worst fashion/beauty/love advice that's ever been given to you? What will finally become of this famous neck of mine? The sky as dark and endlessly translucent as a tapestry. The nocturnal owl and common birds such as canaries. Little wild animals as well, rabbits, squirrels. I have no idea how to sew, or spin cotton. I rely on illustrations from engravings and books as stand-ins for the actual creatures. Or sometimes just memories. If you already know the ending, why bother reading the book? Down the aisle of lime trees, your taillights disappear.

Shadow Box

This is a routine that I made up myself
because it utilizes every part of the body.
Almost like a window. You ask if it's
snowing outside and I say *No. Blossoming.*
Yellow-glowing. Like a good dancer. You
do it on both sides. These whales do not
have teeth. They are the oldest true fossils.
To be recorded on 35 mm. It's expensive.
A cut-out of gray pasted against. Sea foam
green and the infinite numbers. The baleen
of the corset bending. I also cheap out on
leggings, scarves, and denim. Increase the
white-space. Is it out of alignment? Is it
leaf-time yet?

Shadow Box

There are always ways for me to assemble,
wear, mix, and customize my clothing. I
had one and you had one. It was reciprocal.
You were a snowfall and I was so dunzo.
Like an object. Small and glass-fronted. A
ball might represent a planet or the luck
associated with playing a game. The men
put on their dance belts. They harpsichord
me. *Pas de deux* me. Rock me like a ship
that is mostly cobweb. How can your
body not be your livelihood? The thought
of you still clinging to me like the screams
of a crying baby. This ocean of menswear.

In France, June

tastes like lime.
I splashed yellow
paint on the countryside
and called it flowers. Fooled you
too. Drank Perrier
from green cans. In France,
if you want lime
ask for a green lemon.
If you want window shopping
lick the windows.

Poem for the Word

When gossamer is
the ugly word, I lie on sheets

all day envisioning large
white spider legs curling

up the sill or loud
people talking on

telephones. What can I tell you.
I could never find the stairs

to the mezzanine, slouching
to the blogs then back

again to the sheets—
a Fahrenheit dream.

Call me
by my Hebrew name: Anemone.

Call me clumsy.
I'll hide me

at the party
in your orange

shirt on those sheets
again. It will be

elegant on accident
during amateur hour.

Café de la Place

Recently I've been writing of the aftermath
before-the-fact. There is a scene
in a movie shot along the Seine and I try
to recapture. That sunlit feeling. Walking
the very same Quai but never can.
Never could find those shoes again,
that perfect pair. I'm not worried
about someone reading this
over my shoulder because I can't even read
my own handwriting and if I turn my head just so
the light will hit my glasses on the inside
and I can people-watch from behind.
I call them all my disciples. I am in a city
with a figurehead above every door, every body
heavy with travel or with blueness grew.
I am sending electric postcards to not you.
A stranger city of strangers.

Poem for the Airplane

The problem with watching movies about air travel is
that in reality you never get to watch yourself take off
from the outside. When I was little I had to board a plane
from the tarmac and grabbed a grownup's hand,
looking up to realize he was not my father
but the man standing in front of my father.
I am told that I started to cry. I am told by many people
that I am funny. I've invented many puns,
some involving taxidermy and archeologists.
You wouldn't believe me if I told you
I fell in love with a long-haired man named Django
who sold me boxes of wine at Trader Joe's.
His long hair was much curlier than mine. Later in traffic
I watched the reflection of a plane fly across
someone's rear window and when I turned right
I was driving beneath it, following its trajectory.
Following an airplane-shaped bruise in the sky.
I started reading science textbooks to learn more
about bruises but found them very unfunny.
Also, can someone please explain atomization? Also,
what does anthropogenic mean? I learned funny-looking
flightless birds are always the first to go.
The dodo never stood a chance. Emus might be next.
The movies always end the same way: a 747 rippling
behind the jet stream of its own hot flight.

I Put a Body On

Like a clever bride
keeping

her skeleton
key close at hand,

reassembling.
I put honey on my body.

There was a tiny bird inside
a tiny gilded cage, meant to be worn

inside my wig. Birdy. Bird brains.
I stuck feathers in the honey.

As with most things, over time
the honey crystallized.

I put a body on my baby. I dressed
my human skull in jewels and flowers.

Shadow Box

Over time I will learn how to trick fate.
Like, if you keep a piece of clothing
long enough. Eventually it will become
fashionable again. Something burning.
When I watched you cross the street in front
of me it was as though I had summoned
you. Or maybe just imagined you. White-
washed. The interiors painted deep blue.
The art of celestial navigation, whether
by sailors or migrating birds. We fell apart.
Because mercury was in retrograde?
Every night a rebirth. You are Columbine
wrapped in ribbons. The next night:
Pierrot chased by moonlight. The next: the
rag-and-bones man.

Shadow Box

Many things seem impossible. Expensive hotel breakfasts. Sunburns on the soles of your feet. The concept that more is more. I am not afraid. I put on my microshorts, a loose t-shirt, a pair of nice flats because heels would have been a little too. Like I'm trying too hard. City of pigeons. Centuries ago dovecotes or *colombiers* were developed as boxes within boxes for the domestic pigeons kept by knights as a sign of prestige. By now I've stopped caring about birds entirely. Seriously though. When I say these shorts are short, I'm not kidding around.

Shadow Box

New meaning accrues to all memories.
Like, look back in time and where was
the desire? I had lost it but you. You could
paint patches with it. A found object you
could hold in your mouth. Tonight I'm
unbuckling the buckle. I'm not impressing
anyone by telling them that *stanza* is Italian
for *room*. Like animals, these motions
we make are instinctual. The imprint
of something I've held so tightly. For so
long. A piece of French cloud I wear on
occasion. I picked it out because it
reminded me of vintage jewelry. What does
it mean to like animals *in a certain way?*
These are the only poems that I write in bed.

I Saw a Voice Outside My Window

It moved. I put on my coat and snow boots
to investigate. When I got outside the voice was cold
and turning purplish. It wanted a small space
to crawl inside of and it didn't want my house.
It kept moving like a see-through swan
swimming down the street and I followed. It turned
a corner so fast I lost it. I walked to the convenience store
and decided to make a picnic. A winter picnic
in the woods. I bought a perfect basket
for all my foodstuffs and started off into the woods
behind the store. There were no crows or squirrels or deer
anywhere. Eventually I came to a river. I sat down
and made a sandwich with jam and cheese. I made up excuses
of why I couldn't go to work. The little river was half frozen
and, Jesus, the apricot jam tasted so good. The voice
reappeared, but this time it was inside a body.

On Silhouettes

4. vt. to cause somebody or something to appear surrounded by light (often passive)

The pigeons built
three nests on top
of Andy's broken air
conditioner. I call them
our pets. Our pet birds
are silhouettes.
Indonesian shadow
puppets. Bicycle wheels.

Long Radio

The world is attractive
and today it is full

of attractive people.
It's also cold.

All of my hats
are lined with rabbit fur.

My arms are long
enough to reach the top

shelf and far-away doors.
For this I am lucky.

Look at this giant mug
I'm holding. Bicycle

or no bicycle I will roll up
my pant leg to show off

my exquisite right ankle.
I am a pregnant woman

wearing clogs. *Long Radio*
is code for *you are very attractive*

in your gray T-shirt
I would marry you here and now.

One day the world will dissolve
itself into a myriad

of hot snowflakes and ask us
to walk outside into it.

When I Dance

I want to give you the shape
of my thoughts. How nail polish
feels before it dries. There
are so many drugs out there.
The fans automatically shut off
when I move out of my hands.
There's a certain drug
people take that makes them
feel like trees. I'm better
at the jerky movements.
Take me to the supermarket
of your hips and I'll build a home.
A darkening. Some days nothing
good happens and I think
I deserve a treat. I develop
a habit of going
to the mall every day
and buying an Orange Julius.
People get into car accidents.
Keep filling the page. When I think
about that tall Styrofoam cup in my hand
well, you don't want to know. When I say
you killed it I could mean so many things.
To tell the difference
examine how I arrange
my teeth at you. I'll give the outlines
and your fists full of crayons.

Forecasting

Finally it was fashionable to tuck our gray
T-shirts into jeans. For most this was flattering.
We went about popping children's balloons
and stealing Dutch bicycles from grannies
to match our various lipsticks. We took off our pants
and got all anachronistic. The extension of neck and black
stockings up to there. Hands made the perpetual OK-sign
and we peered through peephole fingers at each other.
We took pride in our ability to properly fold
and read newspapers on the train, could sing you
all 88 prepositions. They went sexy on us, so much
so that we wore them out. Instead of focusing our eyes
on one fixed point we softened our gaze and
called it Mountain Vision. We festooned our bouffants
with cocktail umbrellas. Vanity forced us to wear patches
of black court plaster on our faces. The affectation
of a mole to contrast our extreme beauty. Such shapes
might be stars, crescents, or even a horse and carriage.
Some of us pocked our faces full of them.

Definitions of Breathing

1) Ice has always been more expensive than water the cost is to put your own feet in your hands, preferably palm to sole, to create a circuit of the body. Press the forehead into the floor for comfort. Think of a cloud of moths. A pantry full of it.

2) *Please dress in flower print this weekend,* you say. Better to tape a thousand yellow daisies to my skin and pretend it's normal.

3) When I photograph you it's more about the blur than the static. Workmen apply the bright copper gutter. The most cloudless lake. The motorboats of morning. A wrench dropping from the roof.

4) Something about the braless-ness of the day making it a piece of a bigger whole. And in a pair of dingy Keds no less. There is no difference between me thinking it and writing it, only the proof of. Hooking my feet together and lifting my hips helps too. Other definitions of breathing include to repeatedly and alternately take in and blow out air in order to stay alive. To say something in a soft voice or secretively. To allow a person or animal, for example, a horse, to pause to rest or catch a breath. To blow softly or move gently.

5) It was necessary to move closer to the cemetery. We told bad jokes for a living but never at the right moment. No longer afraid of ghosts. They either do not exist or they do and are people. They are just invisible people.

6) I'm not listening to you. I'm wearing my listening face. The sky is vague but I am discrete. Certain as a mathematical equation. Each time I say *pull the shoulders back, shine the heart through* I mean it a little less.

7) You've been modifying your manipulation of movement and I appreciate that. In the way you appreciate how strange clouds look from above, airplane-style. Over the speakers the flight attendants remind us it doesn't matter if you can't get the footwork as long as you clap or snap at the right time.

8) You don't have to drag me back to the city. To the night that is not, but bright. I can recalculate the floors and make this ours. You can buy the hothouse flowers from the corner. I'll check it off the to-do list like that new-haircut feeling. I feel you warming.

Shadow Box

One has to create a narrative to make
sense of this. The orange blossoms full
of bees. Endless suppers. The realization
that my body could be something new
to someone. Every pound of me buzzing.
Shaved and dressed and ready for the
evening. This box might function as a
bouquet. An accumulation. It might
include the phrase *Homage to the Romantic
Ballet*. Even with all of this blossoming.
Nobody sees me here. Is thinking of me
right now. As ghosts and memories are
synonymous, I must be something else.

Shadow Box

Repetition is necessary. It evens out the
body. I watch the Atlantic Ocean even out
the evening. Presing silence into. Some-
where in the world you are moving and
the steps you take bring you closer to or
farther from me. If only slightly. What
can I do with this room but remember it?
I am getting better. Something imaginary.
I've been advised to hold my sadness
in my hands like a ball. To observe it.
Something invisible. Fields of poppies.
Fields of wild. Lavender. In the Petit
Trianon. Everyone dressed in white.

Shadow Box

This one is coming to you on its belly.
Sleepless, star-heavy. Almost like a burden
of fruit. I become a substitute or bottomless.
You ask if it's OK and I say *Yes*. Now I
know, I am not waterproof. Something like
I gave you. A thousand civilities. Limes and
oranges. I slip on something black. And a
pair of heels that stand out. If you could
paint an orgasm. This is what it would look
like: wind again. I mistake it for your car in
the drive. I take down my hair. I take my car
to the field, the snow. Fills in between the
lines. Of broken. Where the orchards were.

Thunderstorms Will Be Near

Do you stay in your car
during severe weather conditions?

The problem with desire is.
These storms may produce

frequent cloud to ground
lightning. I want to take you like a taste

of wine before buying the bottle.
Like testing spaghetti

I will throw you
against the wall. For your safety

get inside when these storms approach.
If I've learned anything

from TV it's that a career in modeling
is so much harder than it looks.

The fortune teller takes my hand.
These X's indicate a flood.

These X's indicate a daughter. Moving Northeast
at 45 MPH. And heavy downpours

along a line extending
from. Everybody

loves a good makeover scene. I remove
my glasses and iron my hair.

We compose it quietly. As well as ponding
of water in poor drainage areas. It seeps

across the screen. It mourns us.
If you are caught outside

stay away from isolated tall objects such as
trees. Avoid open areas such as. This

is a work of poetry; any resemblance
to actual events or persons

is entirely coincidental.
The car windows fog.

I slip back.
I slip my shoe off.

Use my toes to write
your name on the pane.

Another Poem for You

We were oxidizing at the same exact rate,
it was incredible. I dressed each gasp
in ribbons and *X*'s. My default position
was ravishing-you-with-passion. That was
then. This is now when we Snow-White it
till morning. My heart. Turning, you ask
What do you call a pale-faced silence
that makes a healing sound? Me. Watch me
translate myself into English. Watch me
take my invisible top off. Things reconfigure,
they settle. I bought you this beautiful
silver espresso machine—it was imaginary
in the best possible sense.

Apologia

Soon you will be living in my bedroom.
I won't be there but I won't be dead.
I've made space for you. I've packed up
all my books and folded up my linens.
The spare key is under the empty flower pot.
Feel free to use my shampoo. You will
hear footsteps overhead but don't worry.
I promise you this is a good house.
The boys upstairs are alive and sometimes
they are loud. There's a fat orange cat
next door. There was an arsonist
who used to light cars on fire in the middle
of the night but now he's in jail.
In the spring the skunks go crazy and scream
and gangbang in the driveway.
You will get used to the fruit moths.
Across the street is a brick house painted sky blue
and they've started stripping the paint but
you can watch the men at work all day
from the kitchen window. I'm sorry. I was lying
when I said that I was not dead.
I'm a ghost wearing my only dress.
You can find me in the perfume. You can
stare at your reflection in the microwave
and repeat my name until I appear.

NOTES

"Horses Dream of Horses" takes its title from an installation of the same name by the artist Urs Fischer. The first couplet is a direct quote by Fischer from the article "The Art of Urs Fischer" by Calvin Tomkins, which appeared in *The New Yorker,* October 19, 2009.

"Husbands & other seasons" is a direct quote from Steven Karl's poem "Endings Are For Novels But You Are Only My Lyric" from *(Ir)Rational Animals* (Flying Guillotine Press, 2010).

The following books provided inspiration and source material for the "Shadow Box" series: *Joseph Cornell's Theater of the Mind: Selected Diaries, Letters, and Files* edited by Mary Ann Caws (Thames & Hudson, 1993); *Joseph Cornell: Shadowplay Eterniday* edited by Lynda Roscoe Hartigan, Walter Hopps, Richard Vine, and Robert Lehrman (Thames & Hudson, 2003); *Dime-Store Alchemy: The Art of Joseph Cornell* by Charles Simic (Ecco Press, 1992); and *Utopia Parkway: The Life and Work of Joseph Cornell* by Deborah Solomon (Farrar, Straus and Giroux, 1997). Ideas and fragments were also borrowed from *Versailles* by Kathryn Davis (Houghton Mifflin, 2002) and from Garance Doré's eponymous fashion blog (www. garancedore.fr/en).

Photo courtesy of Carly Gaebe

Lily Ladewig is a graduate of Tufts University and the MFA Program for Poets and Writers at the University of Massachusetts Amherst. Her poems have appeared in *Conduit, Denver Quarterly, H_NGM_N, Salt Hill,* and *SUPERMACHINE.* With Anne Cecelia Holmes she coauthored the e-chapbook *I Am A Natural Wonder* (Blue Hour Press, 2011). She lives in Brooklyn, NY.